SWEDEN 2016 HUMAN RIGHTS REPORT

EXECUTIVE SUMMARY

The Kingdom of Sweden is a constitutional monarchy with a freely elected multiparty parliamentary form of government. Legislative authority rests in the unicameral parliament (Riksdag). Observers considered the national elections in 2014 to be free and fair. In the same year, the king announced that the center-left coalition led by Stefan Lofven of the Social Democratic Party had taken office. The king is largely a symbolic head of state. The prime minister is the head of government and exercises executive authority.

Civilian authorities maintained effective control over the security forces.

The main human rights abuses included societal discrimination and incidents of violence against foreigners, particularly the large numbers of migrants who arrived since 2015 and members of ethnic and religious minorities, and domestic abuse of women and children. Authorities subjected a high percentage of pretrial detainees to extended periods in isolation and limited their access to visitors, mail, and exercise.

Other problems reported during the year included shortcomings in the government's processing, sheltering, and integrating the large number of asylum seekers and migrants; increasing numbers of displaced migrant children living on the streets; an increased number of anti-Semitic hate crimes; trafficking of men, women, and children; and sometimes forced street begging by socially excluded Roma.

Authorities generally prosecuted officials who committed abuses in the security services or elsewhere in the government.

Section 1. Respect for the Integrity of the Person, Including Freedom from:

a. Arbitrary Deprivation of Life and other Unlawful or Politically Motivated Killings

There were no reports that the government or its agents committed arbitrary or unlawful killings.

b. Disappearance

There were no reports of politically motivated disappearances.

c. Torture and Other Cruel, Inhuman, or Degrading Treatment or Punishment

The constitution and law prohibit such practices, although there were sporadic reports of police using excessive force.

On February 17, the Council of Europe's Committee for the Prevention of Torture (CPT) released a report on its 2015 visit to the country in which it reported receiving some accusations, including from juveniles younger than 18, of police use of excessive force during apprehension. The allegations mainly concerned the unjustified use of pepper spray, truncheon blows, violent pushing of the apprehended person to the ground, tight handcuffing, and lifting a detainee by the handcuffs. The CPT also received one allegation of physical mistreatment (consisting of punches) while the person concerned was inside a police station. As a result, the person reportedly sustained injuries that required immediate hospitalization.

Prison and Detention Center Conditions

There were no significant reports regarding serious prison, detention center, or migrant detention facility conditions that raised human rights concerns.

Physical Conditions: During 2014, the latest year for which data were available, there were three reports of suicide by prisoners.

In its February 17 report, the CPT noted that many foreign nationals it interviewed at the Norrtalje Prison complained they were sometimes locked in their cells for 23 hours a day for two to three days in a row as unofficial collective punishment following a fight between two or more inmates.

While the CPT reported that conditions in cells at remand prisons were generally good, it noted that none of the cells at the Kronoberg Remand Prison and hardly any of the cells at the Falun Remand Prison had in-cell sanitation. While the majority of prisoners interviewed stated that they had ready access to a toilet facility (including at night), the CPT received a few complaints about delays (on occasion, up to three hours) in gaining access to the toilet, especially at Falun.

<u>Independent Monitoring</u>: The government permitted monitoring by independent, nongovernmental observers, including the CPT. While the national Red Cross and church associations may visit prisoners, they may not monitor or inspect the prisons.

d. Arbitrary Arrest or Detention

The constitution and law prohibit arbitrary arrest and detention, and the government generally observed these prohibitions.

Role of the Police and Security Apparatus

The national police and the national criminal police are responsible for law enforcement and general order within the country. The Security Service is responsible for national security related to terrorism, extremism, and espionage. The Ministry of Justice provides funding and letters of instruction for police activities, but it does not control how they were performed. According to the constitution, all branches of the police are independent authorities.

Civilian authorities maintained effective control over the national police, the national criminal police, and the Security Service, and the government had effective mechanisms to investigate and punish abuse and corruption. The CPT noted that the government had created an Internal Investigation Department within the police force and strengthened its independence. There were no reports of impunity involving the security forces during the year.

Civilian authorities maintained effective control over the national police and the national criminal police, and the government has effective mechanisms to investigate and punish abuse and corruption. There were no reports of impunity involving the security forces during the year.

Arrest Procedures and Treatment of Detainees

The law requires warrants based on evidence and issued by duly authorized officials for arrests. Police must file charges within six hours against persons detained for disturbing public order or considered dangerous and within 12 hours against those detained on other grounds. Police may hold a person six hours for questioning or as long as 12 hours, if deemed necessary for the investigation, without a court order. After questioning, authorities must either arrest or release an individual, based on the level of suspicion. If a suspect is arrested, the prosecutor has 24 hours (or three days in exceptional circumstances) to request continued detention. Authorities must arraign an arrested suspect within 48 hours and begin initial prosecution within two weeks unless there are extenuating circumstances. Authorities generally respected these requirements.

Although there is no system of bail, courts routinely released defendants pending trial unless authorities considered them dangerous or there was a risk the suspect would leave the country. Detainees may retain a lawyer of their choice. In criminal cases the government is obligated to provide an attorney, regardless of the defendant's financial situation.

The law affords detainees prompt access to lawyers and to family members. A suspect has a right to legal representation when the prosecutor requests his detention beyond 24 hours (or three days in exceptional circumstances). Regarding access to a lawyer, the CPT observed that it was usually granted at the beginning of the first formal interview by the investigating officer, although the CPT received a few allegations of delayed access, including until the very end of the police custody period. The CPT stated that its observations suggested it was still highly exceptional for persons in police custody to benefit from access to a lawyer from the very outset of deprivation of liberty (i.e., from the moment they were obliged to remain with police). The type of crime that authorities accused a suspect of committing influenced the suspect's access to family members. Authorities sometimes did not allow a suspect any contact with family members if police believed it could jeopardize an investigation.

Restrictive conditions for prisoners held in pretrial custody remained a problem, although the law includes the possibility of appealing a decision to impose specific restrictions to the Court of Appeals and ultimately to the Supreme Court. According to the Swedish Prison and Probation Service, during the year authorities subjected approximately 66 percent of pretrial detainees to extended isolation or to restrictions on mail delivery or exercise. Authorities stated they took this step when detainees' contact with individuals outside the detention center could risk destroying evidence or changing witnesses' statements, thereby imperiling a continuing investigation.

In its February 17 report, the CPT noted "a lack of progress" in correcting the problem of detention in isolation since its previous visit in 2009 and regretted "that despite 24 years of on-going dialogue between the CPT and the Swedish authorities on the matter, there are no real signs of progress as regards the widespread imposition of restrictions on remand prisoners." It stated the number of remand prisoners subject to restrictions had dropped by only 2 percent in five years. The restrictions consisted of an almost total absence of organized activities, with most remand prisoners spending up to 23 hours per day alone in their cells, sometimes in an isolation cell, with hardly anything to occupy themselves. The report noted the deleterious psychological effect on detainees of prolonged curtailments on contact with the outside world. It recommended that remand prisons "spend a reasonable part of the day outside their cells, engaged in purposeful activities of a varied nature."

Detainee's Ability to Challenge Lawfulness of Detention before a Court: Persons arrested or detained, whether on criminal or other grounds, are entitled to challenge in court the legal basis or arbitrary nature of their detention and to obtain prompt release and compensation if found to have been unlawfully detained.

Protracted Detention of Rejected Asylum Seekers or Stateless Persons: The Migration Board had five closed detention centers to hold foreign nationals deprived of their liberty under aliens legislation. The centers had a combined capacity of 255 persons. In August the centers held in custody 202 persons who were waiting to be deported.

e. Denial of Fair Public Trial

The constitution and law provide for an independent judiciary, and the government generally respected judicial independence.

Trial Procedures

The constitution provides for the right to a fair public trial, and an independent judiciary generally enforced this right.

Defendants enjoy a presumption of innocence, have a right to be informed promptly and in detail of the charges against them (with free interpretation as necessary from the moment charged through all appeals), and have a right to a fair, public trial without undue delay. Defendants may be present at their trial. Cases of a sensitive nature, including those involving children, rape, and national security, may be closed to the public. In other cases, judges or court-appointed civilian representatives decide guilt or innocence. Defendants have the right to be present at their trial and to consult an attorney in a timely manner. In criminal cases, the government is obligated to provide a defense attorney. Defendants generally have adequate time and facilities to prepare their defense. Defendants and their attorneys have access to government-held evidence relevant to their cases. Defendants may confront or question witnesses against them and present witnesses and evidence on their behalf. They may not be compelled to testify or confess guilt. If convicted, defendants have the right of appeal. The law extends the above rights to all defendants.

Political Prisoners and Detainees

There were no reports of political prisoners or detainees.

Civil Judicial Procedures and Remedies

Individuals and organizations may seek civil remedies for human rights violations in the general court system. Citizens may appeal cases involving possible violations of the European Convention on Human Rights by the government to the European Court of Human Rights.

f. Arbitrary or Unlawful Interference with Privacy, Family, Home, or Correspondence

The constitution and law prohibit such actions, and there were no reports that the government failed to respect these prohibitions.

Section 2. Respect for Civil Liberties, Including:

a. Freedom of Speech and Press

The constitution provides for freedom of speech and press, and the government generally respected these rights. An independent press, an effective judiciary, and a functioning democratic political system combined to promote freedom of speech and press.

Freedom of Speech and Expression: The law criminalizes expression considered to be "hate speech" and prohibits threats or expressions of contempt for a group or member of a group based on race, color, national or ethnic origin, religious belief, or sexual orientation. Penalties for hate speech range from fines to a maximum of four years in prison. In addition, the country's courts have held that it is illegal to wear xenophobic symbols or racist paraphernalia or to display signs and banners with inflammatory symbols at rallies.

In 2015 there were reports of 552 cases involving hate speech, or 11 percent of all hate crimes reported. Of the hate crime cases reported in 2014, the last year for which detailed information was available, approximately 46 percent were investigated, 49 percent were dismissed without an investigation, and 4 percent led to prosecution.

Press and Media Freedoms: The law criminalizing "hate speech" applies as well to print and broadcast media, the publication of books, and online newspapers and journals.

Internet Freedom

The government did not restrict or disrupt access to the internet or censor online content, and there were no credible reports the government monitored private online communications without appropriate legal authority. According to the Swedish Institute, more than 95 percent of the country's residents between the ages of eight and 55 percent used the internet on a daily basis. Approximately 90 percent of the population had broadband connectivity in their homes.

Academic Freedom and Cultural Events

There were no government restrictions on academic freedom or cultural events.

b. Freedom of Peaceful Assembly and Association

The constitution provides for the freedoms of assembly and association, and the government generally respected these rights.

c. Freedom of Religion

See the Department of State's *International Religious Freedom Report* at www.state.gov/religiousfreedomreport/.

d. Freedom of Movement, Internally Displaced Persons, Protection of Refugees, and Stateless Persons

The constitution and law provide for freedom of internal movement, foreign travel, emigration, and repatriation, and the government generally respected these rights.

<u>Abuse of Migrants, Refugees, and Stateless Persons</u>: Police reported that since 2012 there were 180 arsons involving housing facilities for asylum seekers. In July the Swedish Civil Contingencies Agency presented a study showing that half of the fires were household accidents, while 11 percent were assaults that involved a "racist intent," the majority of which were aimed at refugee housing facilities with no individuals present.

In its February 17 report, the CPT reported receiving allegations that prison staff imposed unofficial collective punishments on detained foreign nationals after fights between two or more such prisoners in special units in the Norrtalje and Storboda prisons. Most detained migrants told the CPT they had not been informed of the reasons for their detention; the CPT found that written information about detention and the rules of the prison were available to the prisoners only in Swedish.

The government cooperated with the Office of the UN High Commissioner for Refugees (UNHCR) and other humanitarian organizations in providing protection and assistance to refugees, asylum seekers, stateless persons, and other persons of concern.

Protection of Refugees

<u>Access to Asylum</u>: The law provides for the granting of asylum or refugee status, and the government has established a system for providing protection to refugees. In November 2015, to cope with the large inflow of refugees and migrants, the government tightened entry standards to the minimal international and EU levels. Applicants may appeal unfavorable asylum decisions.

Up to July the country received 17,687 asylum seekers. In 2015 a total of 162,877 persons applied for asylum, of whom 43.2 percent were under 18 years of age. Slightly more than half of the minors applying for asylum came without a legal guardian. The large number of asylum seekers was an impediment to the expeditious processing of asylum applications. Since the Migration Agency needed approximately one year to process an application for asylum, excluding appeals, many cases adjudicated during the year concerned persons who applied in previous years. During the year until July, the average time for processing a case was 317 days. In 2015 the corresponding figure was 229 days.

During its visits in 2009 and 2015, the CPT found that the law provides for a public defense counsel to be appointed for detained foreign nationals who are subject to an expulsion or refusal-of-entry order, but only concerning the problem of detention and if the person concerned has been detained for more than three days. A public defense counsel is also not provided to persons who have been refused entry to the country and were detained by police, unless the detention period exceeds three days. The CPT also understood that persons deported under the Dublin Regulation could not benefit from a public defense counsel. Based on these findings, the CPT stated that it would appear that the right of access to a lawyer for persons detained under the country's aliens legislation is unduly limited.

Safe Country of Origin/Transit: In accordance with EU regulations, the government denied asylum to persons who had previously registered in other EU member states or in countries with which the country maintained reciprocal return agreements. During the year the Migration Agency decided to return 7,937 such persons to those countries, excluding Greece. Many of those persons remained in the country during their appeals. In August police had 3,153 cases of individuals who refused to leave the country voluntarily and 7,422 cases of persons who remained after their asylum claim was denied.

Access to Basic Services: A new law entered into force on July 20 limiting asylum seekers' possibilities of being granted residence permits and the possibility for the applicant's family to be allowed to come to the country. The law states that asylum seekers who have been denied residence in the country are no longer entitled to asylum housing or a daily allowance. The Migration Board reported on July 1 that by then 2,400 persons lost the right to social services and 1,700 were forced to leave their asylum accommodation.

According to the nongovernmental organization Human Rights Watch, approximately 35,000 unaccompanied minors entered the country in 2015. The organization alleged that many of the children did not receive health checks, psychosocial counseling and support, or timely meetings with social workers. Some experienced delays of more than three months in being assigned a legal guardian and enrolling in school. Processing each child's request for asylum could reportedly take as long as two years.

The February 17 CPT report noted there was no systematic medical screening of detained migrants upon arrival at the Marsta detention center or assurance of medical confidentiality.

Durable Solutions: The government authorized financial support for the repatriation of asylum seekers denied residence in the country in the amount of

30,000 kronor ($3,280) per adult and 15,000 kronor ($1,640) per child, with a maximum of 75,000 kronor ($8,200) per family. In 2015 the government provided repatriation support to 216 persons, most of them of Iraqi origin.

Temporary Protection: The government also provided various forms of temporary protection to individuals who may not qualify as refugees. In 2015 it provided humanitarian protection to 12,746 persons, subsidiary protection to 18,180 persons, and temporary protection to 396 persons.

Stateless Persons

According to UNHCR, there were 31,062 stateless persons in the country in December 2015. The large number of stateless persons was due to the influx of migrants and refugees and the birth of children to stateless parents who remained stateless until either one parent acquired citizenship or a special application for citizenship (available for stateless children under the age of five) was made. Most stateless persons came from the Middle East (the Occupied Territories, Lebanon, Syria, and Iraq) and Somalia.

Stateless persons who are granted permanent residence may obtain citizenship through the same naturalization process as other permanent residents. Gaining citizenship generally takes four to eight years, depending on the individual's grounds for residency, ability to establish identity, and lack of a criminal record.

Section 3. Freedom to Participate in the Political Process

The constitution provides citizens the ability to choose their government in free and fair periodic elections held by secret ballot and based on universal and equal suffrage.

Elections and Political Participation

Recent Elections: Observers considered the national elections held in 2014 to be free and fair.

Participation of Women and Minorities: No laws limit the participation of women and members of minorities in the political process, and women and minorities did participate.

Section 4. Corruption and Lack of Transparency in Government

The law provides criminal penalties for corruption by officials, and the government generally implemented the law effectively. There were isolated reports of government corruption during the year.

Financial Disclosure: The law requires public officials and political parties to disclose income and assets. The declarations are available to the public, and there are criminal and administrative sanctions for noncompliance.

Public Access to Information: The constitution and law provide for public access to government information, and the government generally granted such access to citizens and noncitizens, including foreign media.

Section 5. Governmental Attitude Regarding International and Nongovernmental Investigation of Alleged Violations of Human Rights

A variety of domestic and international human rights groups generally operated without government restriction, investigating and publishing their findings on human rights cases. Government officials were often cooperative and responsive to their views.

Government Human Rights Bodies: The country had seven national ombudsmen: four justice ombudsmen; the chancellor of justice; the children's ombudsman; and the discrimination ombudsman with responsibility for ethnicity, gender, transsexual identity, religion, age, sexual orientation, and disabilities. There were normally ombudsmen at the municipal level as well. The ombudsmen enjoyed the government's cooperation and operated without government or party interference. They had adequate resources, and observers considered them generally effective.

Section 6. Discrimination, Societal Abuses, and Trafficking in Persons

Women

Rape and Domestic Violence: Rape, including spousal rape, and domestic violence are illegal, and the government enforced the law effectively. The law stipulates more severe penalties for repeated crimes and for cases in which the perpetrator had a close relationship with the victim. Penalties range from two to 10 years in prison. The National Council for Crime Prevention (NCCP) reported 5,920 rapes in 2015, the latest year for which data were available, compared with 6,697 rapes in 2014.

Authorities apprehended and prosecuted abusers in most cases of domestic violence. The majority of women subjected to domestic violence never pressed formal charges against the perpetrator.

The law provides for protection of survivors from contact with their abusers. When necessary, authorities helped survivors protect their identities or obtain new identities and homes. According to the latest available official statistics, 13,109 persons, mostly women, were in these programs as of 2014. Both national and local governments helped fund volunteer groups that provided shelter and other assistance for abused women, and both private and public organizations ran shelters and operated hotlines.

Female Genital Mutilation/Cutting (FGM/C): The law prohibits FGM/C. There were no official reports of FGM/C on women. In January 2015 the National Board of Health and Welfare estimated that approximately 38,000 women, including 7,000 children, from 27 Middle Eastern and African countries and living in the country might have been subjected to FGM/C. The estimate did not include women who arrived in the most recent immigration influx.

Other Harmful Traditional Practices: Honor-related violence often involved immigrants from the Middle East or South Asia. No information was available regarding the extent of honor-related violence. In June 2015, the latest available data, the Swedish Prison and Probation Services estimated that 73 persons were in prison for committing honor-related violence.

Sexual Harassment: The law prohibits sexual harassment, and the government generally enforced this law. In 2015, 8,840 sexual harassment cases were registered, a decrease of 8 percent compared with 2014. In 79 percent of the cases, the victim was a girl or a woman. Criminal penalties range from a fine to up to two years in prison.

Reproductive Rights: Couples and individuals have the right to decide the number, spacing, and timing of their children; manage their reproductive health; and have access to the information and means to do so, free from discrimination, coercion, or violence.

Discrimination: Women have the same legal status and rights as men, including under family, religious, personal status, labor, property, nationality, and inheritance law. The law requires equal pay for equal work. Women's salaries averaged approximately 88 percent of those of men. Women were underrepresented in high-ranking positions in both the public and the private sectors (see section 7.d.).

Gender-based discrimination in access to credit, owning or managing a business, and access to education and housing is prohibited and was not commonly reported.

Children

Birth Registration: Citizenship is derived from one's parents. Children born in the country, regardless of their parents' citizenship and status in the country, were registered immediately in the tax authority's population register.

Child Abuse: Child abuse was a problem. The law prohibits parents or other caretakers from abusing children mentally or physically. Parents, teachers, and other adults are subject to prosecution if they physically punish a child, including by slapping or spanking. The usual sentence for such an offense is a fine combined with counseling and monitoring by social workers. Authorities may remove abused children from their homes and place them in foster care.

The NCCP reported approximately 20,800 child abuse offenses in 2015. Of these, 37 percent were against girls and 63 percent against boys. There was a 9 percent increase in the number of reported assaults on children between 2014 and 2015.

The children's ombudsman published a number of reports and publications for children and those working to protect children from abuse.

Early and Forced Marriage: The minimum age of marriage is 18, and it is illegal for anyone under 18 to marry. The law allows no exceptions.

Female Genital Mutilation/Cutting (FGM/C): Information is provided in the women's section above.

Sexual Exploitation of Children: The law criminalizes "contact with children under 15 for sexual purposes," including internet contact intended to lead to sexual assault. Penalties range from fines to one year in prison. The law prohibits the sale of children; penalties range from two to 10 years in prison. It also bans child pornography with penalties ranging from fines to six years in prison. Authorities enforced the law. The minimum age for consensual sex is 15.

<u>Displaced Children</u>: On November 17, Stockholm's County Council presented a report commissioned by the government showing that, from 2013 to May, 1,829 children, or 4 percent of all unaccompanied minors, went missing after being assigned to a county reception home. Most of the missing children were boys. Algeria and Morocco, countries from which only a low percentage were granted asylum, were overrepresented. The report suggested the fear that their asylum application would be rejected and they would be deported was the leading reason for the disappearances. Some children left their assigned reception counties to go to another county--often to larger cities--in the country. Children who were about to reach the age of 18 or who had their age upgraded in the asylum process were also overrepresented in the statistics.

Stockholm Police reported that underage children, mainly from Morocco, Algeria, and other countries in North Africa, were living on the streets. Police estimated that approximately 800 boys were criminally active, a majority of them in Stockholm and Gothenburg, without residency and without a legal guardian in the country. Many children sought asylum in the country, but authorities considered only a much smaller number as qualifying for asylum. Social Services offered accommodation for children or foster families regardless of asylum status, but many were stuck in a criminal lifestyle. Because in many cases the juveniles' countries of origin were unwilling to accept them back due to their criminal record, they could not be deported. In May the Swedish and Moroccan governments agreed to initiate a joint committee to try to resolve the problem.

<u>International Child Abductions</u>: The country is a party to the 1980 Hague Convention on the Civil Aspects of International Child Abduction. See the Department of State's *Annual Report on International Child Abduction* at <u>travel.state.gov/content/childabduction/en/legal/compliance.html</u>.

Anti-Semitism

Leaders of the Jewish community estimated there were 20,000 to 30,000 Jews in the country and approximately 6,000 registered members of a Jewish congregation. The NCCP registered 277 anti-Semitic crimes in 2015, compared with 267 in 2014, an approximately 4 percent increase. This was the highest number of anti-Semitic crimes since 2009 and included threats, verbal abuse, vandalism, graffiti, and harassment in schools. Anti-Semitic incidents were often associated with events in the Middle East and actions of the Israeli government, and Swedish Jews were at times blamed for Israeli policies.

The most common forms were unlawful threats/harassment (46 percent), hate speech (37 percent), defamation (6 percent), and vandalism/graffiti (5 percent). Eight violent anti-Semitic hate crimes were reported in 2015, a decrease of 33 percent on the year.

Authorities initiated an investigation in 55 percent of the cases reported in 2014; 45 percent were directly dismissed due to lack of evidence. Formal charges were brought in only 3 percent of the cases.

In June the Board of State Aid to Religious Communities approved a grant of 1.2 million kronor ($131,000) to Swedish Jewish congregations to improve their security. The grant was earmarked for the hiring of additional security guards.

On May 31, a court in the southern city of Malmo convicted an 18-year-old man of a hate crime directed at a local Chabad rabbi. The perpetrator was fined 2,000 kronor ($219)--determined as a proportion of the man's income--for the crime of "harassment with a hate crime motive." In April 2015 the perpetrator yelled profanities from a passing car at the rabbi and his family as they were walking to synagogue. The rabbi had previously reported at least 50 similar incidents to police since moving to Malmo in 2004. The case was the first in which harassment directed against the rabbi reached the courts.

Police, politicians, media, and Jewish groups have stated that anti-Semitism has been especially prevalent in Malmo. The Simon Wiesenthal Center left in place its travel warning, first issued in 2010, regarding travel in southern Sweden, because Jews in Malmo could be "subject to anti-Semitic taunts and harassment."

In June, five 15-year-old boys were fined for hate speech in the Ystad District Court for performing a Nazi salute in a photograph at school. The principal reported the incident to police. Two of the boys appealed the decision, citing the limited distribution of the photo.

In August the Raoul Wallenberg Academy presented its national school project, "Every person can make a difference," that sought to inform students about human rights and equality.

The Swedish Civil Contingencies Agency continued to cooperate with religious communities on a national level to promote dialogue and prevent conflicts leading to anti-Semitic incidents. It continued to train police officers to detect hate crimes and visited high schools to raise awareness of such crimes and encourage more victims to report abuses. The government made available information in several languages for victims of hate crimes and provided interpreters to facilitate reporting. Police hate-crime units existed throughout the country.

Trafficking in Persons

See the Department of State's *Trafficking in Persons Report* at www.state.gov/j/tip/rls/tiprpt/.

Persons with Disabilities

The law prohibits employers from discriminating against persons with physical, sensory, intellectual, and mental disabilities in hiring decisions and prohibits universities from discriminating against students with disabilities in making admission decisions. The law protects, and the government effectively enforced, the right to access to healthcare and other public services. The law also prohibits discrimination in the judicial system and air travel and other transportation.

In 2015 the number of reports of discrimination against persons with disabilities in employment, education, access to health care, or the provision of government services increased to 680, compared with 461 in 2014. Of the cases, 297 concerned access limitations. Those involved handled many complaints through mediation procedures rather than formal court hearings.

Inadequate accessibility of all kinds for persons with disabilities is a violation of the law. Observers reported cases of insufficient access to privately owned buildings used by the public, such as apartments, restaurants, and bars. Many buildings and some means of public transportation remained inaccessible. Government regulations require full accessibility for new buildings, and similar requirements exist for public facilities.

National/Racial/Ethnic Minorities

The law recognizes Sami (formerly known as Lapps), Swedish Finns, Tornedalers, Roma, and Jews as national minorities. The discrimination ombudsman received 663 complaints regarding ethnic discrimination in 2015, compared with 601 in 2014.

Societal discrimination and violence against immigrants and Roma continued to be problems during the year.

Police registered reports of xenophobic crimes, some of which were linked to neo-Nazi or white power ideology. Police investigated and the district attorney's office prosecuted race-related crimes. Official estimates placed the number of active neo-Nazis and white supremacists at 1,500. Neo-Nazi groups operated legally, but courts have held that it is illegal to wear xenophobic symbols or racist paraphernalia or to display signs and banners with inflammatory symbols at rallies, since the law prohibits incitement of hatred against ethnic groups.

Expo, a private foundation that researches and maps antidemocratic, right-wing extremists and racist tendencies in the country, reported increased radicalization in society. Neo-Nazi dissemination of mainly online propaganda increased, but such groups were still marginalized due to the violence of their activists.

The government estimated the Romani population at 50,000. A majority of the Roma lived as socially excluded outcasts. The unemployment rate among Roma was high, due in part to poor education and prejudices. In 2015 authorities identified 240 hate crimes directed against Roma, including several acts of violence. Perpetrators of nonviolent hate crimes usually worked in the service sector, as civil servants, or were unknown to the victim. The number of Roma, mainly from Romania, engaged in street begging increased. As EU citizens, they are allowed to stay in the country without permission for up to three months; begging is legal.

On January 26, the Council of Europe's commissioner for human rights, Nils Muiznieks, sent a letter to Culture Minister Alice Bah Kuhnke concerning the reported eviction of approximately 200 persons, mostly Romanian and Bulgarian Roma, in the Sorgenfri district of Malmo in November 2015. Muiznieks noted that the city offered emergency accommodation for five days to only approximately 50 of the persons affected. Responding to Muiznieks, the minister for children, the elderly, and gender equality, Asa Regner, confirmed the basic facts but asserted that the persons evicted occupied approximately only half of the accommodations offered by authorities.

On June 10, the Stockholm District Court ruled that the government was guilty of ethnic discrimination in a suit brought by 11 individuals (eight adults and three children) who were included in the illegal Skane County police register of the country's Roma. The court awarded the litigants 30,000 kronor ($3,280) each, stating in its decision that, "There is strong reason to believe that inclusion in the register was solely based on their ethnicity. The state has not presented sufficient evidence to prove there were any other reasons for the registration." The government appealed the decision.

In June the Commission against "Antiziganism" created shortly after the Skane County registration scandal presented a report to the minister for culture and democracy. The report included recommendations to offer an official apology to the country's Roma for human rights violations of the past and to start a national center to continue to work for Romani rights.

The government continued its 20-year strategy to equalize the opportunities available to young Roma and non-Roma by 2032. The strategy included a series of measures to improve the condition of Roma in six focus areas: education, work, housing, health and social care, culture and language, and civil society. On October 7, the government announced it earmarked 58 million kronor ($6.34 million) for Roma inclusion work for 2016-19. The Agency for Youth and Civil Society Affairs and the Swedish Arts Council received new assignments to support Romani organizations both financially and in other ways. Among the actions already taken is the work of three pilot municipalities--Gothenburg, Helsingborg, and Linkoping--that have instated permanent consultation procedures when it comes to problems concerning the Romani group. The National Agency for Education has developed material for working with national minorities at the local level, and the National Board for Health and Welfare has worked with an education project for the social services. The Roma Youth Association initiated projects for Romani youth, including a student fund to help young students through school.

The Gothenburg City Museum's exhibition, "We are Roma--Meet the People Behind the Myth" opened in Malmo in October. The exhibition examined why Roma were not accepted into society. The Forum for Living History arranged workshops and education on human rights for schoolchildren, companies, government authorities, and associations.

Indigenous People

The approximately 20,000 Sami in the country are full citizens with the right to vote in elections and participate in the government, including as members of the country's parliament. They are not, however, represented as a group in parliament. A 31-member elected administrative authority called the Sami parliament ("Sametinget") also represented Sami. The Sami parliament acted as an advisory body to the government and had limited decision-making powers in matters related to preserving the Sami culture, language, and schooling. The national parliament and government regulations governed the Sami parliament's operations.

Longstanding tensions between the Sami and the government over land and natural resources persisted, as did tensions between the Sami and private landowners over reindeer grazing rights. Certain Sami have grazing and fishing rights, depending on their tribal history. The Sami continued to press the government for exclusive access to grazing and fishing.

In June the District Court in Gallevare fined a 20-year-old man for hate speech after he made racist comments about the Sami on his Facebook page. The case marked the first time someone was convicted for hate speech aimed at the Sami.

Acts of Violence, Discrimination, and Other Abuses Based on Sexual Orientation and Gender Identity

Antidiscrimination laws exist, apply to lesbian, gay, bisexual, transgender, and intersex (LGBTI) individuals, and were enforced. There were isolated incidents of societal violence and discrimination against persons perceived to be LGBTI. The NCCP reported 600 hate crimes based on sexual orientation and 60 reports of transphobic hate crimes.

Other Societal Violence or Discrimination

In 2015 the NCCP identified more than 6,980 police reports with a hate crime motive, the highest level to date. The increase was due to a rise in vandalism and graffiti cases that entailed xenophobic motives.

Section 7. Worker Rights

a. Freedom of Association and the Right to Collective Bargaining

The law provides for the right of workers to form and join independent unions, bargain collectively, and conduct legal strikes. The government respected these rights. The law prohibits antiunion discrimination, and a worker may not be fired because of union activity. If a worker were unlawfully fired for union activity, the case would go to court. If the court found the dismissal unlawful, the employee would have the right to be reinstated. The parties may also negotiate until they find a solution that satisfies both sides.

Foreign companies may be exempt from collective bargaining provided they meet minimum working conditions and pay. Public-sector employees enjoy the right to strike, subject to limitations in the collective agreements protecting the public's immediate health and security. The government mediation service may also intervene to postpone a strike for up to 14 days for mediation. The International Trade Union Confederation claimed the law restricts the rights of the country's trade unions to take industrial action on behalf of foreign workers in foreign companies operating in the country. The law allows unions to conduct their activities largely without interference. The Labor Court settles any dispute that affects the relationship between employers and employees. An employer organization, an employee organization, or an employer who has entered into a collective agreement on an individual basis may lodge claims. The Labor Court may issue prison sentences of up to three years, and they were sufficient to deter violations. Administrative and judicial procedures were not subject to lengthy delays and appeals.

Workers and employers exercised all legal collective bargaining rights, which the government protected. The government and employers respected freedom of association and the right to collective bargaining. There were few reports of antiunion discrimination and violence toward union members.

b. Prohibition of Forced or Compulsory Labor

The law prohibits all forms of forced or compulsory labor, including by children, and the government effectively enforced the law. Penalties ranged from two to 10 years in prison and were comparable with other serious violations. Forced labor involving trafficked men and women occurred in agriculture, construction, hospitality, domestic work, and forced begging and theft. Women and children were also sometimes trafficked for the sex trade. There were reports of forced labor involving trafficked children (see section 7.c.). In some cases employers or contractors providing labor seized the passports of workers and withheld their pay. Resources and inspections were adequate.

Also see the Department of State's *Trafficking in Persons Report* at www.state.gov/j/tip/rls/tiprpt/.

c. Prohibition of Child Labor and Minimum Age for Employment

The law permits full-time employment from the age of 16 under the supervision of local authorities. Employees under the age of 18 may work only during the daytime and under supervision. Children as young as 13 may work part time or perform light work with parental permission. The government effectively implemented these laws and regulations. The law limits the types of work children may or may not engage in. For instance, a child may not work with dangerous machinery or chemicals. A child may also not work alone or be responsible for handling cash transactions. No cases of child labor were reported. Illegal employment of a child in the labor market is considered a civil rather than a criminal violation. According to law, forcing a child to work may be treated as coercion, deprivation of liberty, or child abuse, and carries a wide range of penalties, including fines and imprisonment. Resources for enforcement were adequate.

Children trafficked from outside the country were subjected to forced begging, forced petty theft, and sexual exploitation. In 2015 the Stockholm County Council presented a new national survey of child victims and suspected victims of trafficking. The survey indicated that 32 children were subjected to trafficking during 2015. Police and social services reportedly acted promptly on these cases.

d. Discrimination with Respect to Employment and Occupation

The law and regulations prohibit discrimination with respect to employment or occupation on the basis of race, color, gender, religion, political opinion, national origin or citizenship, social origin, disability, sexual orientation, gender identity, age, language, or HIV-positive or other communicable diseases status. The government generally enforced these laws effectively. Unlawful discrimination may result in a fine or time in prison according to the law.

Discrimination in employment or occupation occurred. The discrimination ombudsman investigated complaints of gender discrimination in the labor market. The ombudsman received 619 complaints of discrimination in the labor market, of which 157 were related to gender. According to *The Economist* on November 5, 5 percent of native-born workers were jobless, while the rate for workers from outside the EU was 22.5 percent. Reasons reported for why employers were reluctant to hire foreign-born workers included uncertainty about their qualifications, their right to work, skeptical public opinion, and language barriers. Approximately 200 of the complaints of ethnic discrimination involved the labor market. Complaints may also be filed with the courts or with the employer. Labor unions generally mediated in cases filed with the employer.

e. Acceptable Conditions of Work

There is no national minimum wage law. Annual collective bargaining agreements set wages. By regulation both foreign and domestic employers must offer conditions of employment on par with the country's collective agreements. Nonunion establishments generally observed these contracts as well.

The legal standard workweek is 40 hours or less. The labor law and collective bargaining agreements regulate overtime and rest periods. The law allows a maximum of 200 hours overtime annually. Collective agreements determined compensation for overtime, which could take the form of money or time off. The law requires a minimum period of 36 consecutive hours of rest, preferably on weekends, over a seven-day period. The law also provides employees with a minimum of five weeks' paid annual leave.

The Swedish Work Environment Authority, a government agency, effectively enforced these standards. In 2015 the authority conducted approximately 21,000 labor inspections. It employed an estimated 260 inspectors around the country, approximately 0.6 inspectors per 10,000 employees. Violators are subject to fines. Information regarding their sufficiency to deter violation was not available.

The Swedish Work Environment Authority issued occupational health and safety regulations, and trained union stewards and safety ombudsmen whom government inspectors monitored. Safety ombudsmen have the authority to stop unsafe activity immediately and to call in an inspector. The authority effectively enforced these rules. Workers may remove themselves from situations that endanger health and safety without jeopardizing their employment, and authorities effectively protected employees in this situation. An employer may be fined up to one million kronor ($109,000) for violating work environment regulations.

A foreign company providing berry pickers to Swedish companies must have a branch registered in the country to guarantee the conditions of employment. The foreign labor broker must also show how it expects to pay workers in case of limited work, such as, for example, a bad berry harvest.

Many foreign seasonal workers, including berry pickers from Asia and Bulgaria, faced harsh conditions of work, including the seizure of passports, withholding of pay, and poor living and working conditions. In 2015 the Swedish Retail and Food Federation presented new guidelines to improve the situation of the pickers. The guidelines cover EU citizens who pick berries in the country but not workers from outside the EU. Under the guidelines berry pickers are to be informed that they have the right to sell their berries to all buyers and that nobody has the right to control their work hours. The guidelines task food and retail organizations with ensuring their implementation. During the year authorities received 3,200 applications from Thailand for work permits to pick berries, compared with 4,000 applications in 2015.